Fun Fan Facts:

The Unofficial NBA Edition

New Orleans Pelicans

Everything Young New Orleans Pelicans Fans Should Know

By: Jake Liam

Dedication

For Grandma Edie -

You do everything for me, and I notice every single bit
of it. This one is yours.

THE NBA
BY THE NUMBERS

MOST NBA CHAMPIONSHIPS*

CELTICS (18) †

LAKERS (17)

WARRIORS (7)

BULLS (6)

SPURS (5)

As of the 2024-25 Season. † One Trophy = 4 Championships.

NBA HISTORY SNAPSHOT

1946 NBA Founded — **1954** Shot Clock Introduced — **1979** 3-Point Line Added — **2023** NBA Cup Introduced

BIG NUMBERS

$156 million
Stephen Curry's est. earnings in the 24-25 season

7'7"
Tallest player in NBA history (Gheorghe Mureşan & Manute Bol)

30 | 4 | 82

30 Teams Competing in the NBA

4 Playoff Rounds

82 Games Per Season

NEW ORLEANS PELICANS
IN THE NBA

- FOUNDED: 2002†
- NBA TITLES: 0
- CONFERENCE TITLES: 0*

10 Playoff Appearances

*† Founding dates are complicated & may cause arguments at Thanksgiving. Ask someone born before color TV. All Titles reflect pre-relocation franchise history. * As of 2024-25 Season.*

NBA ALL-TIME MVP LEADERS

KAREEM ABDUL-JABBAR (6) ★ MICHAEL JORDAN (5) ★ BILL RUSSELL (5)

EASTERN CONFERENCE

Atlantic – **Celtics**
Atlantic – **Nets**
Atlantic – **Knicks**
Atlantic – **76ers**
Atlantic – **Raptors**
Central – **Bulls**
Central – **Cavaliers**
Central – **Pistons**
Central – **Pacers**
Central – **Bucks**
Southeast – **Hawks**
Southeast – **Hornets**
Southeast – **Heat**
Southeast – **Magic**
Southeast – **Wizards**

WESTERN CONFERENCE

Pacific – **Lakers**
Pacific – **Clippers**
Pacific – **Warriors**
Pacific – **Suns**
Pacific – **Kings**
Northwest – **Nuggets**
Northwest – **Timberwolves**
Northwest – **Thunder**
Northwest – **Trail Blazers**
Northwest – **Jazz**
Southwest – **Mavericks**
Southwest – **Rockets**
Southwest – **Spurs**
Southwest – **Pelicans**
Southwest – **Grizzlies**

Introduction

Welcome, fans! Whether you're new to cheering for the New Orleans Pelicans or you've been bleeding the team colors your whole life, this book is packed with fun, exciting facts about your favorite team. Get ready to impress your friends and family with everything you know about the New Orleans Pelicans.

Quick Timeout

This book is packed with stats. Like, A LOT of stats. Every fact was checked, double-checked, and triple-checked. But here's the thing about basketball history: not everyone agrees on everything. Ask someone who watched games before color TV and someone who grew up with instant replay and you'll get two completely different answers. My dad, stepdad, uncle, and grandpa all argued about the same fact. Four people. Four answers. All of them think they're right. So if you spot something that doesn't match what you've heard, congratulations. You might be a bigger fan than the people who helped make this book. And honestly? That's pretty cool.

HOW IT WORKS

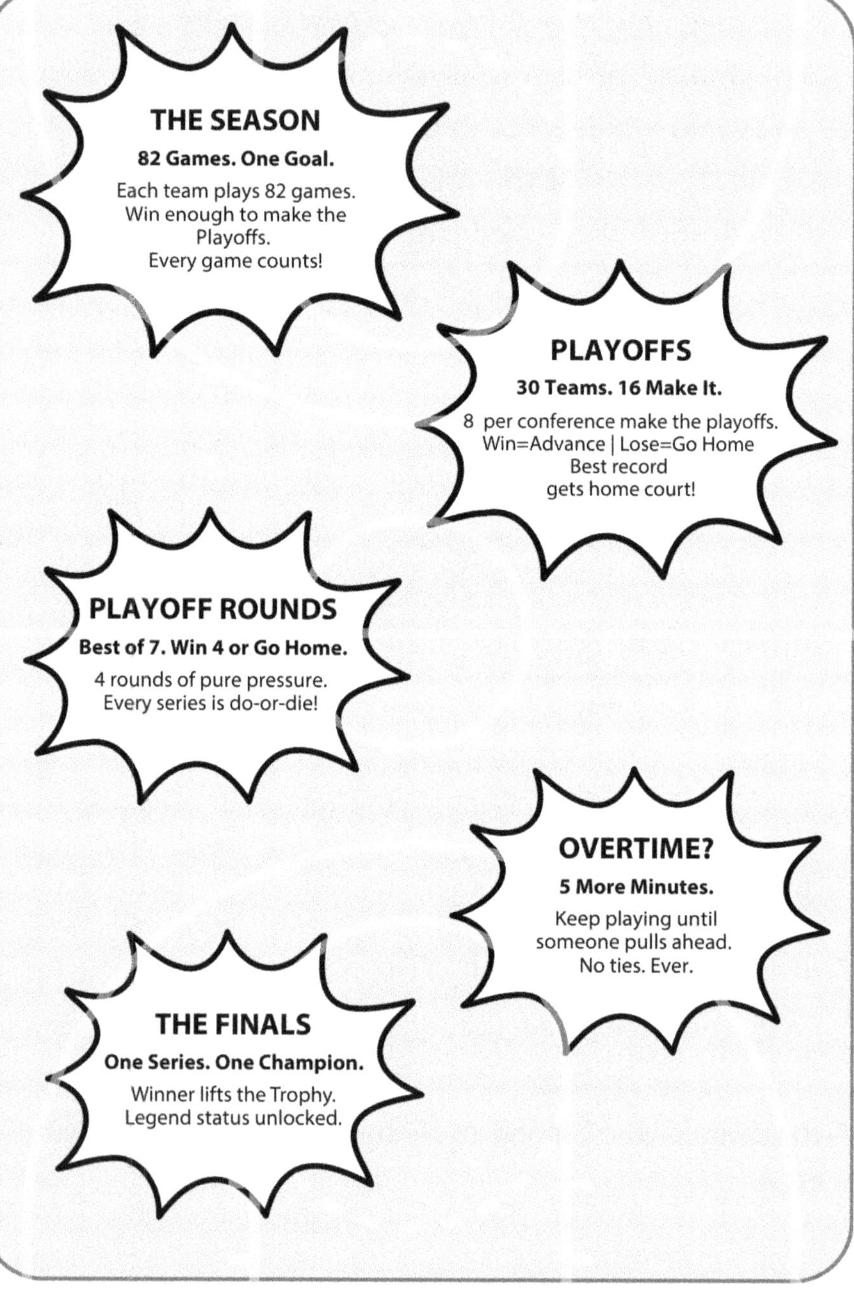

THE SEASON

82 Games. One Goal.

Each team plays 82 games.
Win enough to make the
Playoffs.
Every game counts!

PLAYOFFS

30 Teams. 16 Make It.

8 per conference make the playoffs.
Win=Advance | Lose=Go Home
Best record
gets home court!

PLAYOFF ROUNDS

Best of 7. Win 4 or Go Home.

4 rounds of pure pressure.
Every series is do-or-die!

OVERTIME?

5 More Minutes.

Keep playing until
someone pulls ahead.
No ties. Ever.

THE FINALS

One Series. One Champion.

Winner lifts the Trophy.
Legend status unlocked.

How the NBA Works

At first glance, basketball feels simple. Ten players. One ball. Two hoops. Go.

Then the NBA adds the layers.

An 82-game regular season. A draft where bad teams pick first. Playoffs that last two full months. Superstars who can change everything with one trade. Dynasties that rise, fall, and rise again.

And somehow, it all works.

The NBA is built on one big idea: every team gets a chance to reset, reload, and rise again. No relegation. No dropping down to a lower league. Just basketball, every night, from October through June.

It is a league designed for drama, stars, and comebacks. And once you understand the flow, it is impossible to stop watching.

The League Setup

The NBA has 30 teams, spread across the United States and Canada. Those teams are split into two conferences:

- Eastern Conference
- Western Conference

Each conference has three divisions, mostly based on geography. Divisions matter for scheduling, but not as much as they used to.

Every team plays 82 regular season games, usually from October through April. Home games. Road games. Back-to-back nights. Long road trips. The season is a marathon before the sprint even starts.

Win games, and you climb the standings. Lose too many, and the pressure builds fast.

How Games Are Played

An NBA game has four quarters, each lasting 12 minutes. That means 48 minutes of game time, plus timeouts, free throws, and the occasional coach argument that adds another 20 minutes nobody planned for.

Scoring is simple:

- A shot inside the three-point line is worth 2 points
- A shot beyond the arc is worth 3 points
- Free throws are worth 1 point

If the score is tied at the end of regulation, the game goes to overtime, which lasts 5 minutes. Still tied? Another overtime. Keep going until someone wins.

There is a shot clock too. Teams have 24 seconds to take a shot. No standing around. No holding the ball forever. Keep it moving.

The Regular Season Race

The regular season is long for a reason. It tests everything.

Depth. Health. Focus. Patience.

Teams play opponents from both conferences, but they face conference rivals more often. By the end of the season, each conference's top teams have earned their playoff spots the hard way.

The goal is simple: make the playoffs. But there is a twist.

The NBA Cup

In 2023, the NBA added something new to the middle of the season. Something with actual stakes. They called it the In-Season Tournament, now known as the NBA Cup.

It works like this: Every team plays a small group stage during November and December, with special court designs that look like nothing else in basketball. The best teams advance to a knockout round held in Las Vegas.

The winners split a prize pool. Players earn bonus money. And for the first time, a team could lift a trophy before the playoffs even started.

Some fans are still warming up to it. Some players love it. But the moment a team starts treating it seriously and a crowd shows up buzzing in December, it feels like something.

Which, honestly, sounds about right.

The Play-In Tournament

Instead of sending the top eight teams from each conference straight to the playoffs, the NBA added something new. The Play-In Tournament.

Here is how it works:

- Teams ranked 1 through 6 in each conference are safe
- Teams ranked 7 through 10 fight for the final two playoff spots

The 7 and 8 seeds have an advantage. Win once and you are in. Lose and you still get one more shot. The 9 and 10 seeds have to win twice in a row just to earn a first-round matchup.

It turns the end of the season into a sprint. Every game suddenly matters more. Fans love it. Coaches age rapidly.

The NBA Playoffs

Once the playoffs begin, everything tightens.

Sixteen teams enter. Eight from each conference. Every round is a best-of-seven games series. That means the first team to win four games moves on:

- First Round
- Conference Semifinals
- Conference Finals
- NBA Finals

Home-court advantage matters. Crowds get louder. Rotations get shorter. Superstars play heavier minutes. One bad quarter can flip a series. One great performance can define a career.

By the time the NBA Finals arrive in June, only two teams are left. One from the East. One from the West. Four wins away from a championship. Four wins away from history.

The NBA Draft: Hope Begins Here

Here is where the NBA gets clever. Every summer, new players enter the league through the NBA Draft. Teams take turns selecting college players, international stars, and teenagers straight out of high school.

The teams that finished with the worst records get the best odds to pick early through the Draft Lottery. It is not guaranteed, but it gives struggling franchises a real shot at changing their future with one pick.

That means one bad season does not doom you forever. It might actually change everything. Some franchises are rebuilt by a single draft night moment.

Hope shows up wearing a new jersey.

No Relegation. All Pressure.

Unlike many global sports leagues, NBA teams never drop down to a lower league. They always stay in the NBA.

That does not mean there is no pressure.

Fans remember losing seasons. Owners make changes. Coaches get replaced. Players get traded. Every year is a test of direction, patience, and belief.

Stars, Systems, and Showtime

The NBA is famous for its stars. But stars do not win alone.

Teams need chemistry. Coaches need systems. Role players need to deliver on the biggest stages. One injury. One hot streak. One trade deadline deal. Any of it can flip a season.

That balance between individual brilliance and team basketball is what makes the league special.

Fast breaks. Buzzer-beaters. Game 7s. And moments that get replayed forever. That is the NBA.

Once you get the flow, it is pure electricity.

New Orleans Pelicans Facts

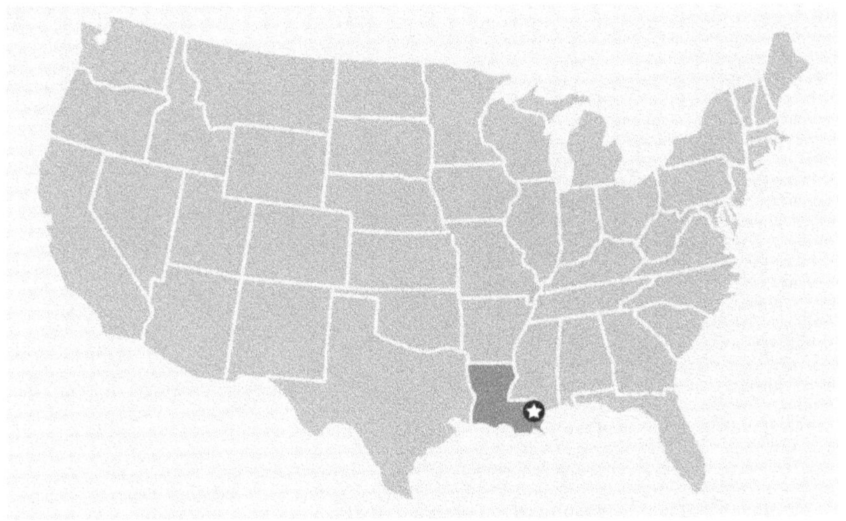

Home City

New Orleans, Louisiana

Metro Area Population

About 1.3 Million

Home Arena

Smoothie King Center

Arena Capacity

16,867

Conference / Division

Western Conference / Southwest Division

Famous Local Food

Beignets, jambalaya, gumbo, crawfish etouffee, po'boys

Chapter 1: From the Bayou to the Big Leagues

1. Born in Charlotte, Raised in New Orleans

Picture this: you are a perfectly normal basketball team playing in Charlotte, North Carolina. You have got fans, a schedule, a logo. Life is fine. Then one day the NBA basically taps you on the shoulder and says, "Hey, New Orleans needs a team. Pack your bags." That is roughly what happened in 2002 when the Charlotte Hornets franchise picked up everything it had and relocated to Louisiana, becoming the New Orleans Hornets.

It was not exactly a smooth transition. Charlotte fans were furious. New Orleans fans were not sure what to think. And the players were probably googling "best beignet spots" between practice sessions. But the move made sense in a big-picture way. New Orleans is one of the most passionate sports cities in America, a place where people celebrate everything with music, food, and a whole lot of noise. Basketball had a real home there, it just needed a little time to figure that out.

The city welcomed the team the way New Orleans welcomes everything: loud, proud, and with a parade somewhere nearby. The Hornets were not perfect yet, but New Orleans did not need perfect. It needed basketball, and finally it had it.

2. The Name Nobody Expected

Here is a fun question to ask your friends: what do pelicans and basketball have in common? They both involve a lot of awkward flapping and the occasional impressive catch. Okay, that is a stretch. But when the team officially became the New Orleans Pelicans in 2013, a lot of people had questions.

The Hornets name had history in Charlotte, and when that city got its expansion team back in 2014, New Orleans needed something new. Rather than go generic, the franchise leaned all the way into Louisiana pride. The pelican is the official state bird, on the flag, on the buildings, basically on everything that is not moving fast enough to escape. Choosing it was the franchise finally saying out loud: we are not a relocated team anymore. We are a Louisiana basketball team.

Whether the name fits is a longer conversation. And it turns out, it is a pretty good one. More on that later.

3. Homeless in the NBA

Imagine showing up to school one day and being told your classroom no longer exists. Now imagine that, but you are an NBA team and your city just got hit by one of the worst natural disasters in American history. That is what happened when Hurricane Katrina devastated New Orleans in August 2005. The storm was catastrophic. The flooding destroyed neighborhoods, displaced hundreds of thousands of people, and left the Smoothie King Center, then called the New Orleans Arena, so damaged it could not be used.

The Hornets had nowhere to play. So they split their home games between Oklahoma City and San Antonio, becoming the most well-traveled team in the league for two full seasons. Oklahoma City, as it turned out, absolutely loved having an NBA team, filling arenas night after night and treating the Hornets like their own. A few years later, the NBA would remember that enthusiasm when it placed a permanent team there.

New Orleans finally came home for the 2007-08 season, and the city showed up. It was more than just basketball coming back. It was a symbol that New Orleans was coming back too. And that season, they

would have a point guard who made sure everyone
noticed.

4. The Expansion That Never Was

Most people assume New Orleans always had a
professional basketball team waiting in the wings. It did
not. For a long time, Louisiana was just not on the
NBA's radar, which is genuinely surprising when you
think about how obsessed the state is with sports.
Football? Obviously. College basketball? Huge. Pro
basketball? The league basically said "not yet" for
decades.

New Orleans had actually been considered for an
expansion franchise multiple times before the Hornets
arrived, but the bids never quite came together. The
city had the fans, it had the culture, it had the food that
would make every road team secretly excited to visit. It
just did not have the arena situation or the ownership
group to make it happen on the league's timeline.

When the Charlotte relocation finally landed the team
in Louisiana, it felt less like a gift and more like an
overdue arrival. New Orleans had been waiting for its
team. It just had to borrow someone else's first.

5. Building on the Bayou

The early New Orleans Hornets roster was not exactly loaded with household names. Baron Davis was the biggest star, a point guard with a highlight reel that could break the internet on a nightly basis. Beyond him, the team was a work in progress, which is a polite way of saying they had some figuring out to do.

But building a team in New Orleans came with some unexpected advantages. The city's energy is contagious. Home games felt like events rather than games, with jazz music, second-line dancers, and fans who treated every possession like it personally mattered to them. Opposing teams noticed. Playing in New Orleans was different from playing anywhere else in the NBA, and that atmosphere became a genuine home-court advantage.

The front office worked through draft picks, trades, and a lot of trial and error in those early years. The team was not a contender yet, but it was learning what it wanted to be. It wanted to be fast, exciting, and impossible to ignore, which, honestly, sounds exactly like the city it plays in.

6. Chris Paul: The Point God (2005-2011)

There are point guards, and then there is Chris Paul. The difference is roughly the same as the difference between a weather app and an actual meteorologist. One gives you information. The other controls the whole situation.

"CP3" (his initials plus his jersey number #3) arrived in New Orleans for the 2005-06 season as the fourth overall pick out of Wake Forest, and within two years he had completely taken over. His 2007-08 season could be one of the greatest individual performances in franchise history. He led the entire NBA in assists and steals simultaneously, which had only been done by a tiny handful of players ever. He was so good at reading defenses that opponents basically had to change their entire game plan just to slow him down, and even then, it usually did not work.

What made Paul special was not just the numbers. It was the control. He made every player around him better, turned a mid-level roster into a playoff contender, and gave New Orleans its first real taste of what a franchise cornerstone could look like. He left for Los Angeles in 2011, and Pelicans fans still bring him up the way you bring up a great meal you had years ago. You know you cannot have it back. You just wish you could.

7. Anthony Davis: The Brow (2012-2019)

The 2012 NBA Draft lottery was one of the most important nights in New Orleans basketball history, and the team did not even have to do anything impressive to make it happen. They just had to win the lottery. Which they did. And with the first overall pick, they selected Anthony Davis out of Kentucky, a 19-year-old center who looked like he had been assembled in a laboratory by scientists who really, really liked basketball.

Davis stood seven feet tall with a wingspan that could theoretically block out the sun, and he moved like someone half his size. In his early seasons he was still developing, but even as a rookie he showed flashes of something genuinely rare. By the time he hit his prime in New Orleans, he was putting up scoring and rebounding numbers that made other NBA big men feel vaguely embarrassed.

The Brow became iconic. The skill set was historic. Davis made five All-Star teams as a Pelican and became the face of the franchise for seven seasons. His departure to Los Angeles in 2019 stung, but his impact on the franchise's identity was permanent. New Orleans learned what it felt like to have a true superstar, and that knowledge shaped everything that came after.

Anthony Davis towers over the court at seven feet tall, one unibrow, and zero interest in anyone's opinion about it. He even trademarked it. Your math homework has more separation than this man's forehead. "The Brow" became

8. Baron Davis: The Original Wild Card (2002-2005)

Before CP3, before The Brow, there was Baron Davis. The man who showed up in New Orleans looking like a highlight reel wrapped in a headband, ready to do something ridiculous on any given Tuesday.

Davis was the Hornets' anchor in those earliest years in Louisiana, a fearless point guard who could score from anywhere, pass through impossible windows, and dunk on players a full foot taller than him without blinking. He was exactly the kind of player a new franchise needs: someone who makes the crowd stand up, who gives the team personality before it has a trophy case. New Orleans did not have a championship yet, but on the nights Baron Davis was cooking, it did not matter.

His stint in New Orleans was brief, but his fingerprints stayed on the franchise. He proved the city could draw real talent, that players would come and give everything they had for those fans. Sometimes a team's history is not about rings. Sometimes it is about the guys who showed up first and made people believe something good was coming.

9. Zion Williamson: The Chosen One (2019-Present)

The hype around Zion Williamson before he played a single NBA minute was unlike almost anything the league had seen in years. He was a six-foot-six, 280-pound power forward who could leap like a guard, sprint like a running back, and finish at the rim with a force that made shot blockers quietly reconsider their career choices. The internet had been obsessed with him since high school. By the time New Orleans won the 2019 lottery and drafted him first overall, the whole basketball world had its eyes locked on Louisiana.

Then he got hurt before he ever played a game, and Pelicans fans spent the first half of his rookie season doing something no fanbase should have to do: watching highlights of a player they technically already had. A knee injury kept him out for 44 games while the rest of the league kept moving. The city waited. The hype did not cool. If anything it got louder, because that is what happens when anticipation has nowhere to go.

When Zion finally stepped on the court in January 2020, New Orleans was ready. The building was ready. The rest of the NBA was watching. What happened next belongs in its own chapter.

10. Peja Stojakovic: The Sharpshooter from Serbia (2006-2010)

Not every legend on this list built his legacy over years of star-studded seasons. Sometimes a player shows up at exactly the right moment, does exactly what the team needs, and earns a permanent spot in the memory bank. Peja Stojakovic was that guy for New Orleans.

Stojakovic arrived in 2006 after stints in Sacramento and Indiana, already known as one of the purest shooters in the league. He had a three-point stroke so smooth it looked like a practice shot even during the fourth quarter of a playoff game. When he joined the Hornets, he gave Chris Paul a legitimate scoring threat on the wing, which made CP3's playmaking even more devastating because defenses could not just collapse on the paint.

He played four seasons in New Orleans and was part of that 2007-08 team that made the second round of the playoffs and genuinely scared people. Peja was not flashy off the court. He did not have a famous nickname or a viral moment that lives forever on social media. He just showed up, knocked down threes at an elite rate, and won fans over the old-fashioned way. Sometimes that is the whole job.

11. The 2008 Playoff Run

For a franchise that had survived relocation, a hurricane, and two seasons of playing in borrowed cities, the 2007-08 playoff run felt like a victory lap before the real victory even arrived. Chris Paul was in the middle of the most dominant point guard season anyone in New Orleans had ever seen up close, and he carried the Hornets to the second round of the playoffs for the first time in franchise history.

In the first round, New Orleans dismantled the Dallas Mavericks four games to one. Dallas had Dirk Nowitzki. Dallas had experience. Dallas did not have an answer for Chris Paul running the show at full speed with something to prove. CP3 was everywhere, distributing, defending, and making the kind of reads that make coaches wonder if their point guard can actually see a few seconds into the future.

The run ended in the second round against the San Antonio Spurs, a team that was basically a basketball finishing school at the time. Losing to San Antonio in 2008 was not embarrassing. It was educational. New

Orleans had announced itself as a real team in a real city with real playoff ambitions, and the rest of the league had officially been put on notice.

12. The Best Season in Franchise History

If New Orleans basketball fans needed proof that their team belonged, the 2007-08 season delivered it in bold, unmistakable fashion. The New Orleans Hornets finished 56-26, the best record in franchise history, and won their first division title in New Orleans franchise history. Chris Paul was electric, finishing second in MVP voting and making opponents look like they were defending a magician who refused to reveal his tricks. David West averaged over 20 points a game. The city, still rebuilding from Katrina, had something to rally around that felt bigger than basketball.

In the first round of the playoffs, the Hornets faced the Dallas Mavericks, who had been NBA Finals runners-up just two years earlier. New Orleans won the series in five games, sending Dallas home and announcing to the league that this was not a fluke. The second round brought the defending champion San Antonio Spurs, who had won four titles and treated playoff runs like a routine Tuesday. The series went to seven games. The

Hornets lost, but not before pushing one of the greatest franchises in NBA history to the absolute limit.

It remains the high-water mark for basketball in New Orleans. The Hornets did not win a championship that year, but they proved something to themselves and to a city that desperately needed proof: this team could compete with anyone.

13. The Night Anthony Davis Scored 59

Most NBA players go their entire careers without scoring 50 points in a single game. On February 21, 2016, Anthony Davis dropped 59 on the Detroit Pistons, along with 20 rebounds. In a single game. A stat line so absurd it sounds like something you would put together in a video game when the difficulty is set to easy. He shot efficiently, he dominated the paint, and he did it all with a calm that made the whole thing somehow more impressive. The Pistons tried everything. Davis tried everything back, and he had more of it.

The 59-point game became an instant franchise landmark and one of the most talked-about individual performances in the league that season. It was the moment a lot of casual basketball fans stopped thinking of Anthony Davis as a promising young big man and started thinking of him as a genuine problem for every team in the NBA. Detroit fans went home that night and stared at the ceiling for a while. New Orleans fans went home and could not stop smiling.

That game made Davis the youngest player ever to score 59 in a game. It put him in company with Shaquille O'Neal and Wilt Chamberlain as the only players in 50 years to record a 55-point, 20-rebound performance. The Pistons had no answer. Nobody did.

14. Zion's Debut and the Winning Streak

The wait had lasted 44 games, which for Pelicans fans felt roughly equivalent to a flight that keeps getting delayed with no explanation while the gate agent makes confident eye contact and says nothing. When Zion Williamson finally suited up on January 22, 2020 against San Antonio, the crowd treated it like a national holiday that had been personally delivered to their doorstep.

He scored 22 points in 18 minutes. Eighteen minutes. Most players use 18 minutes to remember what city they are in. Zion used them to remind the entire league why the hype had never actually gone away. He was physical, fast, and finishing at the rim in ways that made defenders look like they were running a different drill entirely. The building lost its mind. Highlights spread before the game was even finished.

New Orleans went on a strong winning run after his arrival, the exact length of which is worth verifying, but the momentum shift was real and visible to anyone watching. The roster woke up. The city fell completely in love. And for those healthy weeks in early 2020, the Pelicans looked like a team that had finally found the piece they had been missing. The question of whether they could hold onto it was a problem for later. For now, Zion was here, and it was everything.

15. The Brandon Ingram Breakout

Brandon Ingram arrived in New Orleans in the Anthony Davis trade, which meant he walked into a city that was still processing the loss of its biggest star. That is not an easy situation for any player to step into. Ingram stepped into it anyway and proceeded to have one of the best individual seasons in franchise history.

In the 2019-20 season, Ingram averaged 24.3 points per game, made his first All-Star team, and won the NBA's Most Improved Player award. He went from being a promising piece in a trade package to being the face of the franchise in under a year, which is a transformation that requires both talent and a certain kind of internal toughness that you cannot coach into someone.

What made Ingram's breakout special was not just the numbers. It was how he carried himself. He was quiet, focused, and consistent in a season that had no shortage of chaos around it. New Orleans needed someone to grab the franchise by the collar and say "I have got this." Ingram did exactly that. He proved that even when a team loses someone great, something new and worth watching can grow in its place.

16. Why a Pelican?

The pelican is not, on paper, an intimidating animal. It does not growl. It does not have claws. Its primary skill is scooping fish into a stretchy throat pouch, which is impressive at a seafood buffet but not exactly the stuff of nightmare fuel. And yet, the pelican is the official state bird of Louisiana, plastered on the state flag, carved into buildings, and beloved by locals in a way that makes perfect sense once you spend five minutes in New Orleans.

Louisiana has had a complicated, beautiful, sometimes heartbreaking relationship with its coastline and waterways for centuries. The pelican represents that connection, a bird that lives on the water, survives storms, and keeps showing up no matter what. Sound familiar? It should, because that is also basically the story of New Orleans itself.

When the team officially became the Pelicans in 2013, some fans rolled their eyes. Pelicans? Really? But give it a few years and the name started to feel inevitable. This is a franchise that survived relocation, survived Katrina, survived rebuilding cycles that would have broken lesser fan bases. A bird that looks a little goofy but refuses to quit? That fits just fine.

17. The Smoothie King Center

The Smoothie King Center is named after a company that sells blended fruit drinks, which is either the most New Orleans thing imaginable or the least, depending on your perspective. Either way, it has been home to Pelicans basketball since the arena opened in 1999, and it has developed a reputation as one of the louder buildings in the NBA on a good night.

The arena seats just under 17,000 fans, which means when the Pelicans are rolling and the crowd is fully locked in, the noise level reaches a point where opposing teams start making communication mistakes. Point guards cannot hear their coaches. Defenses get confused. Road teams suddenly develop an urgent need to call timeout and collect themselves, which the home crowd treats as a personal victory.

New Orleans fans do not attend games to politely observe. They attend games to participate, loudly and continuously, in a way that makes the arena feel more like a second line parade than a sports venue. Other cities have loud arenas. New Orleans has the Smoothie King Center, which is loud and also smells faintly of mango.

18. Mardi Gras and Basketball

In most NBA cities, the regular season schedule is just the regular season schedule. In New Orleans, the regular season schedule runs directly through Mardi Gras, which is the city's annual reminder that it does not require a reason to celebrate, but it will absolutely use one if you offer it.

Mardi Gras in New Orleans is not a one-night event. It is a weeks-long citywide commitment to parades, costumes, beads, music, and food that borders on organized chaos. The Pelicans have learned to lean into this rather than fight it. Home games during the Mardi Gras window have featured themed nights, special promotions, and a general atmosphere that makes every other franchise's promotional calendar look extremely boring by comparison.

There is something genuinely unique about being an NBA team in a city where the local culture is this specific and this overwhelming. It means the Pelicans do not have to manufacture personality. The city provides it for free, every single season, with a brass band and a float.

19. Pierre the Pelican: The Mascot That Broke the Internet

In 2014, the Pelicans unveiled their new mascot. His name was Pierre. He was a pelican. And he looked like something that had escaped from a fever dream and somehow gotten access to a basketball uniform.

The original Pierre design featured enormous human-style teeth, wide unsettling eyes, and the general energy of a character who absolutely should not be left alone with children. The internet reacted the way the internet always reacts to a mascot that crosses the line between friendly and deeply concerning: with absolute delight. Pierre went viral immediately, collected into lists of the scariest sports mascots ever created, celebrated as an unintentional masterpiece of nightmare design.

The Pelicans quietly gave Pierre a makeover shortly after. The new Pierre is friendlier, softer, more conventionally mascot-shaped. He no longer looks like he is planning something. The original Pierre, however, lives forever in the internet's memory as proof that sometimes the most famous thing about a rebrand is the mistake you made on the first try. Rest in peace, original Pierre. You were genuinely terrifying and we miss you.

20. The Pelicans' Wild Uniform History

The New Orleans Pelicans have gone through more uniform looks than most people change their phone cases, and roughly the same percentage of them were questionable decisions in the moment that somehow look better in hindsight.

The early years featured the Charlotte Hornets teal, which did not exactly scream Louisiana. Then came various Hornets-era looks, then the transition to Pelicans branding in 2013, which introduced navy, gold, and red in combinations that took some getting used to. The team has since leaned into its Louisiana identity with alternate uniforms inspired by Mardi Gras colors, jazz culture, and local artistic traditions that actually look spectacular on the court.

The best uniforms in Pelicans history are the ones that stopped trying to look like every other NBA team and started looking like New Orleans. When the colors and the fonts and the design language say "this could only be from Louisiana," something clicks. The city has one of the richest visual cultures in America. The uniform history of this franchise is basically the story of the team slowly figuring out it should just embrace where it lives.

21. Zion's Road Back

Zion Williamson's relationship with the injury report has been, to put it diplomatically, extremely frustrating for everyone involved. To put it less diplomatically: Pelicans fans have spent more time refreshing medical updates than watching him play, which is not a situation anyone signed up for when he went first overall in 2019.

The injuries have been real, the setbacks significant, and the questions about long-term durability have followed him through every season. Weight management, conditioning, and the physical toll of being a 280-pound athlete who plays with the recklessness of someone who has genuinely never heard of taking a night off, all of it has been part of the Zion conversation in a way that no highlight reel can paper over. There have been seasons that felt like extended previews. There have been returns that looked like the real thing before something went sideways again. It has been a lot.

But here is the fact that does not change regardless of the injury timeline: when Zion Williamson is healthy and locked in, he remains one of the most physically dominant players on the planet. The talent is not the question. The ceiling has not moved. New Orleans is still waiting for a full, healthy, fully committed Zion season from start to finish. When it finally arrives, the rest of the NBA should probably start preparing now, just to get a head start on the panic.

22. CJ McCollum: The Steady Hand

CJ McCollum arrived in New Orleans at the trade deadline in February 2022, coming over from Portland in a deal that was designed to give the Pelicans a veteran scorer who knew how to run an offense without accidentally setting it on fire. He delivered immediately and then kept delivering, which is exactly what you want from a player brought in to be the adult in the room.

McCollum is the kind of player who does not show up on casual highlight reels because his brilliance is slightly harder to package into a ten-second clip. He gets to his spots. He finishes through contact. He makes the right read at the right moment with a consistency that makes the game look less like improvisation and more like something he planned out the night before.

Off the court, McCollum has been a genuine community presence in New Orleans, investing in the city and engaging with its culture in ways that go well beyond the standard player-in-a-new-city press conference promises. He showed up and meant it. Pelicans fans noticed, and they have returned the appreciation generously.

23. The Young Core Taking Shape

Every franchise dreams about having young players develop faster than expected. The Pelicans have been living that dream with a core group that has quietly become one of the more intriguing collections of talent in the Western Conference.

Herb Jones arrived as a second-round pick in 2021 and immediately became one of the best perimeter defenders in the league, which is not supposed to happen with second-round picks. Second-round picks are supposed to play ten minutes, look confused, and maybe stick around as a depth piece. Herb Jones apparently did not read that memo. Trey Murphy III developed his three-point shooting to a level that makes him a genuine spacing weapon alongside Zion in the frontcourt. Jose Alvarado, another under-the-radar pick, became a fan favorite for his relentless energy and a defensive intensity that makes opposing ball handlers deeply uncomfortable.

This group is young enough to still be improving, experienced enough to not be surprised by big moments, and collectively cheap enough on the salary cap that the front office has room to maneuver. In NBA terms, that is a genuinely exciting situation to be in.

24. New Orleans as an NBA Destination

For most of the franchise's history, New Orleans had a reputation as a place where stars came through rather than a place where stars chose to go. Free agents looked at the market size, looked at the championship history, and quietly signed elsewhere while pretending the weather was the issue.

Something has been shifting. The city's profile has grown enormously over the past decade. New Orleans has become one of the most desirable destinations in America for food, culture, and general quality of life, which players notice because players are human beings who also enjoy eating well and living somewhere interesting. The Pelicans have invested heavily in their facilities and their organizational culture, and the results have started showing up in conversations around the league.

Landing Zion first overall was the opening move. Building a young roster around him was the second. Convincing the broader basketball world that New Orleans is a place where a star can thrive and be happy is the ongoing project, and the evidence is slowly trending in the right direction. The Pelicans are no longer a consolation prize destination. They are becoming a real option, which in NBA free agency terms, is a very big deal.

25. The Championship Dream

New Orleans has never won an NBA championship. The city knows what a championship feels like, because the Saints won the Super Bowl in 2010 and the celebration lasted approximately three years. The Pelicans have watched that happen from across the city and have been quietly taking notes.

The ingredients for a title run exist in New Orleans in a way they have not always existed before. A generational talent in Zion when healthy. A veteran scorer in McCollum who has been deep in playoff series. A young core that is still ascending. A fan base that would throw the loudest, most musically spectacular championship parade in the history of professional sports, and this is not even a debate.

The window is not fully open yet, but it is no longer firmly closed either. It is cracked, and through that crack you can hear something that sounds a lot like a brass band warming up just in case. New Orleans has been patient with this franchise through relocations and hurricanes and rebuilding seasons and injury updates. When this city finally gets its NBA title, the party will be so good that even the opposing team's fans will probably show up. That is not a threat. That is just New Orleans being New Orleans.

Bonus Trivia Quiz!

You think you are a true New Orleans Pelicans fan? Try this bonus quiz!

1. What year did the Charlotte Hornets relocate to New Orleans?

A) 2000

B) 2002

C) 2005

D) 2008

2. Where did the Hornets play their home games after Hurricane Katrina devastated New Orleans?

A) Houston and Memphis

B) Dallas and Atlanta

C) Oklahoma City and San Antonio

D) Nashville and Baton Rouge

3. What is the official state bird of Louisiana that inspired the team's current name?

A) The Egret

B) The Heron

C) The Pelican

D) The Flamingo

4. In what year did the team officially become the New Orleans Pelicans?

A) 2010

B) 2011

C) 2012

D) 2013

5. Chris Paul was selected with what pick in the 2005 NBA Draft?

A) First overall

B) Second overall

C) Fourth overall

D) Eighth overall

6. Which college did Chris Paul attend before entering the NBA?

A) Duke

B) Wake Forest

C) North Carolina

D) Kentucky

7. Anthony Davis was drafted out of which university?

A) Louisville

B) Duke

C) Kansas

D) Kentucky

8. How many points did Anthony Davis score in his legendary 2016 game against the Detroit Pistons?

A) 50

B) 54

C) 59

D) 62

9. How many rebounds did Anthony Davis grab in that same record-breaking game?

A) 12

B) 15

C) 18

D) 20

10. In the 2008 playoffs, the Hornets eliminated which team in the first round behind Chris Paul's dominant performance?

A) The San Antonio Spurs

B) The Los Angeles Lakers

C) The Dallas Mavericks

D) The Phoenix Suns

11. How many games into his rookie season did Zion Williamson finally make his NBA debut?

A) 24 games

B) 33 games

C) 44 games

D) 52 games

12. Brandon Ingram arrived in New Orleans as part of the trade for which departing superstar?

A) Chris Paul

B) Zion Williamson

C) Anthony Davis

D) Baron Davis

13. What award did Brandon Ingram win during his breakout 2019-20 season?

A) Defensive Player of the Year

B) Most Improved Player

C) Sixth Man of the Year

D) Rookie of the Year

14. Which Pelicans player arrived as a second-round pick and immediately became one of the best perimeter defenders in the league?

A) Trey Murphy III

B) Jose Alvarado

C) Herb Jones

D) CJ McCollum

15. What is the name of the Pelicans' home arena?

A) Caesars Superdome

B) Smoothie King Center

C) Lakefront Arena

D) Bayou Sports Center

Super Fan Secret Challenge

Only a true New Orleans Pelicans fan will know this.

(No Answer Provided)

The New Orleans Pelicans mascot Pierre became viral for his original terrifying design in 2014. Describe what made the original Pierre so unsettling that the team had to redesign him, and name two specific features that fans found disturbing.

Answer Key

1. B) 2002

2. C) Oklahoma City and San Antonio

3. C) The Pelican

4. D) 2013

5. C) Fourth overall

6. B) Wake Forest

7. D) Kentucky

8. C) 59

9. D) 20

10. C) The Dallas Mavericks

11. C) 44 games

12. C) Anthony Davis

13. B) Most Improved Player

14. C) Herb Jones

15. B) Smoothie King Center

NBA PLAYOFF BRACKET

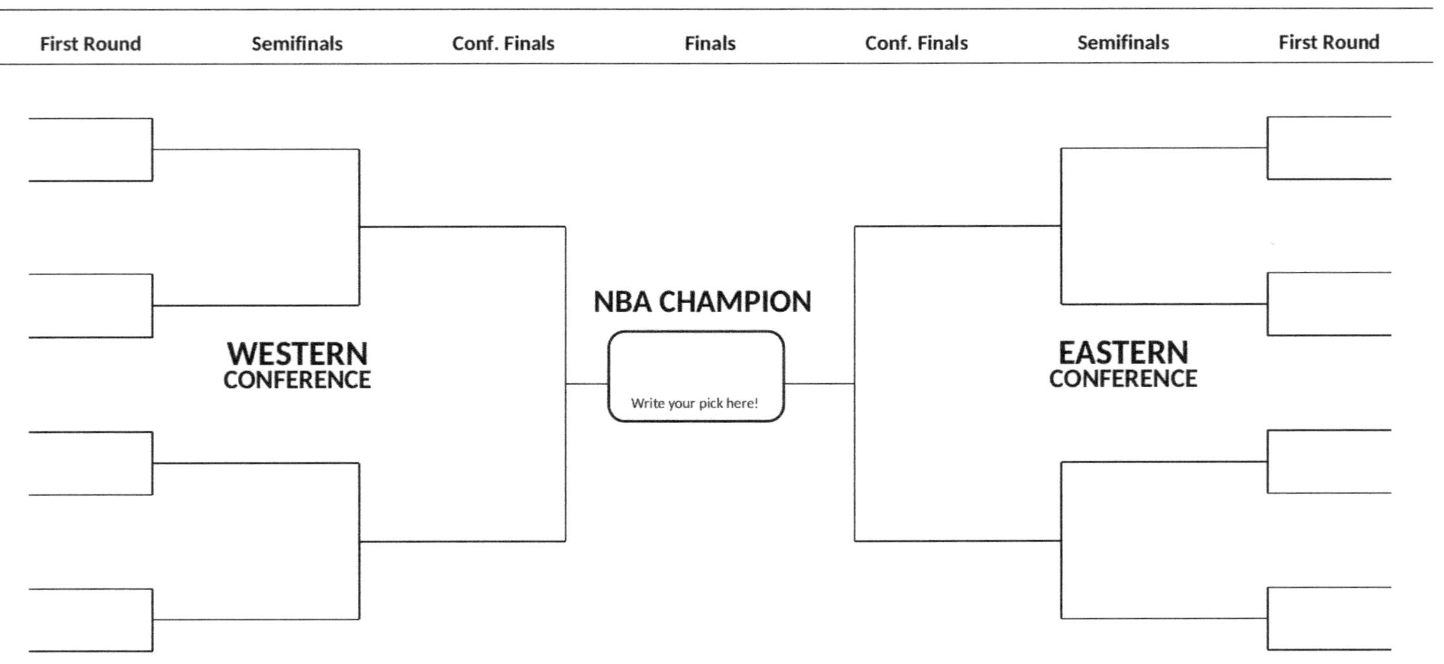

* Fill in your picks and try not to argue with your friends about it!

Part of the Fun Fan Facts: The Unofficial Sports Guide Series

Be the Boss of the Playoffs

You've broken down the matchups. You know which superstar takes over in the fourth quarter. You've seen the bench units that quietly decide series. You've watched the adjustments coaches make when their backs are against the wall.

Now it's time to stop watching and start deciding.

On this page, you are not just a fan. You are the Head Coach drawing up the last play with three seconds left on the clock. You are the GM who built this roster. You are the analyst who saw it all coming.

This is not just filling out a bracket.

This is building your championship run.

Sixteen teams enter the NBA Playoffs. The path is brutal. Best of seven. No shortcuts. No hiding. Every round gets louder, harder, and more personal.

This bracket is your Playoff Control Room.

The Game Plan

1. Survive Round One: Start with the opening round. Which matchup is going seven games? Who has the closer? Who folds under pressure? Make the calls.

2. Feel the Momentum: As you move into the Conference Semifinals and Conference Finals, things change. Role players become heroes. Stars feel the weight. Trust your reads.

3. Own the Finals: Trace your picks all the way to the NBA Finals. When the confetti falls and the trophy is raised, you'll find out who earned it.

House Rules: Circle your boldest upset. That is your official "I knew it" moment.

Choose Your Weapon: Pencil if you want flexibility. Pen if you trust your instincts. Sharpie if you believe in chaos.

Because once the playoffs tip off, there is no rewinding Game 7.

Make your picks. Trust your basketball brain. And let the playoff drama begin.

Fun Facts Wrap-Up

You made it through! You're officially a true superfan! Now it's time to put your knowledge to the test. Share these facts with friends and see who really knows their team best.

Love the series?

Your reviews help other fans discover Fun Fan Facts. If you enjoyed this book, we'd really appreciate you sharing your thoughts and leaving a review.

Want more Fun Fan Facts?

Scan the QR code below to visit our site and explore bonus trivia, challenges, and special extras - including new teams, future series, and collectible fun as they're released.

Collect All the Fun Fan Facts Series!

Check off every book you read. See the full set on Amazon. Search "Fun Fan Facts Jake Liam."

World Cup 2026 Edition

☐ Algeria   ☐ Scotland   ☐ Morocco

☐ France   ☐ Brazil   ☐ Switzerland

☐ Paraguay   ☐ Ivory Coast   ☐ Curaçao

☐ Argentina   ☐ Senegal   ☐ Netherlands

☐ Germany   ☐ Canada   ☐ Tunisia

☐ Portugal   ☐ Japan   ☐ Ecuador

☐ Australia   ☐ South Africa   ☐ New Zealand

☐ Ghana   ☐ Cape Verde   ☐ United States

☐ Qatar   ☐ Jordan   ☐ Egypt

☐ Austria   ☐ South Korea   ☐ Norway

☐ Haiti   ☐ Colombia   ☐ Uruguay

☐ Saudi Arabia   ☐ Mexico   ☐ England

☐ Belgium   ☐ Spain   ☐ Panama

☐ Iran   ☐ Croatia   ☐ Uzbekistan

World Cup 2026 Group Edition

☐ Group A   ☐ Group F   ☐ Group K

☐ Group E   ☐ Group J   ☐ Group D

☐ Group I   ☐ Group C   ☐ Group H

☐ Group B   ☐ Group G   ☐ Group L

English Football Edition

☐ Arsenal F.C.   ☐ Manchester City
☐ Aston Villa F.C.   ☐ Manchester United
☐ Chelsea F.C.   ☐ Newcastle United F.C.
☐ Everton F.C.   ☐ Tottenham Hotspur
☐ Fulham F.C.   ☐ West Ham United
☐ Liverpool F.C.   ☐ Wrexham A.F.C.

NBA Edition

☐ Atlanta Hawks   ☐ Miami Heat
☐ Boston Celtics   ☐ Milwaukee Bucks
☐ Brooklyn Nets   ☐ Minnesota Timberwolves
☐ Charlotte Hornets   ☐ New Orleans Pelicans
☐ Chicago Bulls   ☐ New York Knicks
☐ Cleveland Cavaliers   ☐ Oklahoma City Thunder
☐ Dallas Mavericks   ☐ Orlando Magic
☐ Denver Nuggets   ☐ Philadelphia 76ers
☐ Detroit Pistons   ☐ Phoenix Suns
☐ Golden State Warriors   ☐ Portland Trail Blazers
☐ Houston Rockets   ☐ Sacramento Kings
☐ Indiana Pacers   ☐ San Antonio Spurs
☐ LA Clippers   ☐ Toronto Raptors
☐ Los Angeles Lakers   ☐ Utah Jazz
☐ Memphis Grizzlies   ☐ Washington Wizards

About the Author

Jake is a 13-year-old sports fan who loves football, American football, and basketball. He plays soccer as a goalie and dreams of one day playing for West Ham United and helping teach kids to love the game. His passion for sports runs in the family - his dad was a professional baseball player, and his stepdad sparked his love for West Ham. Through the Fun Fan Facts series, he shares the fun and excitement of sports with fans everywhere.